THE HOW AND WHY WONDER BOOK OF
DESERTS

Written by Felix Sutton
Illustrated by Robert Doremus
Editorial Production: Donald D. Wolf

Edited under the supervision of
   Dr. Paul E. Blackwood, Washington, D. C.
Text and illustrations approved by
   Oakes A. White, Brooklyn Children's Museum, Brooklyn, New York

SCHOOL EDITION

Charles E. Merrill Books, Inc.
By special arrangement with Wonder Books, Inc.

Introduction

The deserts of the world are somewhat of a mystery to most of us. If we know one desert well, we tend to attribute its characteristics to all deserts. This is where we make our mistake, for as this *How and Why Wonder Book of Deserts* makes clear, deserts differ in fascinating ways.

Of course, all deserts have in common a shortage of water. That is what makes deserts. Plants and animals faced with life in a barren environment have worked out wonderful and amazing ways of life in their struggle for existence. Surprising things happen — and in a hurry — to the seeds of wild flowers and other plants when rain falls. Animals also have made remarkable adaptations that permit them to live in the midst of desert conditions.

Man, too, has managed to live on most of the world's deserts. In this book, you will find ample evidence of human ingenuity, reflected in how the challenge of terrible extremes of heat, drought, wind, and sand has been met and conquered.

The deserts of today have not always been deserts. The deserts of today will not always be deserts. Changes through geological time have turned forests and seas into deserts. But changes in the immediate future will more likely be made by man rather than by the relentless forces of Nature, for mankind has learned how to bring water to the desert. He may soon be able to control rainfall and even find other ways to increase the supply of water to the deserts and so transform desert wastelands into blooming gardens that will feed our exploding populations.

This *How and Why Wonder Book of Deserts* will be an important addition to the home or school library.

Paul E. Blackwood

Dr. Blackwood is a professional employee in the U. S. Office of Education. This book was edited by him in his private capacity and no official support or endorsement by the Office of Education is intended or should be inferred.

Library of Congress Catalog Card Number: 65-21504

First Printing

Contents

THE DESERT WASTELAND 3
What causes deserts? 3
Why are deserts near the Equator so hot by day and so cold by night? 6
Where are the world's great deserts? 7

WATER IN THE DESERT 10
What causes desert water holes and oases? 11
What is a mirage? 11

THE FACE OF THE NORTH AMERICAN DESERT 14
How do wind and water sculpture the desert? 15
How was the Petrified Forest formed? 15
What is the Painted Desert? 16
What made the salt deserts? 16
How was the Grand Canyon created? 17

THE PEOPLE OF THE DESERT 18
How do the Bedouins live? 19
Who are the blue-veiled Tuaregs? 21
Who are the Mozabites? 22
Who are the Bushmen? 24
Where do the Bindibu live? 26
Who inhabits the Asian deserts? 26
Who lives on the Atacama? 27
Who lives in the American desert? 28

PLANTS OF THE DESERT 30
What are drought-evaders and drought-resisters? 30

ANIMALS OF THE DESERT 34
Does the camel store water in its hump? 34
What are some typical outback animals? 35
What are the typical animals of the American desert? 36
Insects 36
Toads and lizards 37
Tortoises and armadillos 39
The desert rodents 39
Desert snakes 41
Desert birds 42
The big animals 43

MAN AND THE DESERT 47
How can man create a desert? 47
How can man reclaim a desert? 48

The Desert Wasteland

To a boy or girl who has grown up in a temperate climate — where the surface of the earth is covered by a lush green carpet of grass and trees, and the bright waters of little streams sparkle in the pleasant sun — the desert seems a dread and fearsome place.

At first glance, the desert wasteland appears almost completely devoid of life. Except for a few shriveled bushes and cactus spines, there seems to be virtually no vegetation in the sandy, rocky ground. Since there are no roots to anchor the soil, the hot, dry winds blow the earth bare and cut the rocks into weird twisted shapes and patterns. Now and then, an eagle or a buzzard wheels by on silent wings through the sky, the only apparent sign of life in an empty, sun-scorched world.

But, as we will see, the desert can be curiously alive with both plant and animal life.

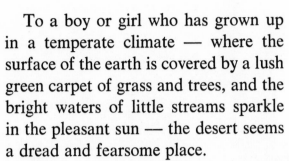

To understand the deserts, we first have to know more about their origin and nature. For quite some time, scientists believed that the deserts were as old as the earth itself. Recently, however, geologists examining rocks, and paleobotanists (the scientists who study the plant life of past geological periods) scrutinizing the fossils embedded in those rocks, with the latest instruments and most advanced means of the atomic age, agree in the opinion that most of our desert regions are no more than one to five million years old; they believe the earth itself to be five billion years old.

There are many ways of defining what a desert is, but as the main characteristic of any desert in the world is dryness, the simplest definition is that it is an area with a rainfall of less than 10 inches during the year. This lack of rainfall is responsible for all the other characteristics of desert regions — the typical vegetation, the animals that live in deserts, and even the way of life of the human inhabitants. Our previous definition of a desert — an area with a yearly precipitation of less than 10 inches — would apply also to the cold regions, or *tundras,* bordering the Arctic Ocean. Our book, however, deals only with the hot, tropical, or low-altitude deserts, and the mid-latitude deserts which occur in the interiors of large continental land masses.

While the lack of rain is, in all instances, the reason for the creation of deserts, the explanation for the lack of rain is not always the same. A look at a map shows that the world's deserts are not scattered at random throughout our planet, but that they are distributed around the globe in two fairly well-

MONUMENT VALLEY, ARIZONA

For 10 months of the year, the deserts of the American West are brown and seared. Then suddenly, they burst into a display of color which is all the more astounding for its contrast with the barrenness of the past season.

defined bands. It is generally agreed that changes in climate or geological structure, or both, are basically responsible for the creation of our arid regions, with the movement of air masses over the surface of the earth the strongest contributing factor. As the earth turns on its axis, the momentum of this movement creates a quite regular pattern of air circulation. This air, which is hot on the Equator, is moving upward and creates a zone of low atmospheric pressure on the Equator. The rising air which flows away on both sides of the Equator, cools off and descends into the two subtropical zones, regions of low atmospheric pressure. Generally, the regions of low atmospheric pressure get

most of the rainfall; in the regions of high atmospheric pressure, the air, which is descending, warms and picks up moisture instead of dropping it in the form of rain.

While these conditions are the major reasons for most of the great deserts in the desert belts of the globe, there are other contributing factors. Some regions become arid because they are far from the sea. Usually, coastal areas are warmer than inland regions. Therefore, when warm, moist winds blow inland, they cool off and lose their moisture on the way, and there is not enough left of life-giving precipitation when they reach the far-off areas. But there are also dry coastal areas which have desert charac-

BARBED-LEAVED ALOE

The famous Camel Corps desert police force was composed mainly of members of the Chamba tribe.

CANDY CACTUS

GIANT SAGUARO

BORREGO DESERT, SOUTHERN CALIFORNIA

Desert flowers, together with flowering cacti, are a feast for the eye.

5

ter. The South American deserts of Peru, Chile, and Argentina, all located very near the ocean, have less than .10-inch rainfall. Responsible for this is the cold Arctic current which chills the damp Pacific winds, condensing their moisture into fog. This fog gets warm while rolling inland. As warm air can carry more moisture, it actually takes up whatever moisture is in the coastal air and blows over these areas, rarely dropping a few drops of rain. Again, lack of rain — desert conditions — as a result.

Another reason for lack of rain can be high mountains, some of which were being created by changes of pressure in our planet within the last 15,000,000 years. The desert lands of the Western United States — the California, Nevada, and Colorado deserts — were created after the Sierra Nevada Mountains were lifted up abruptly on the western edge of the continent and diverted the moisture-bearing winds that blow in from the Pacific Ocean. Moisture-carrying winds lose their moisture moving against and over high, cool mountain ranges.

In some instances, many of the mentioned factors — not just one — work together to cause the lack of rain which makes deserts.

In most non-desert areas of the world, **Why are deserts near the Equator so hot by day and so cold by night?** much of the sun's heat which reaches the lower strata of the atmosphere and the surface of the earth during the day is absorbed by bodies of water or vegetation. Much of it, however, has been deflected by the same cloud cover (the portion of the sky covered by clouds) which prevents the warm air from escaping too rapidly at night. Twenty per cent is deflected by clouds, 10 per cent by dust particles, and 30 per cent by water surface and vegetation. At night, 50 per cent of the heat escapes. About 20 per cent is deflected by clouds; 10 per cent, by dust particles; 20 per cent is held by water and vegetation.

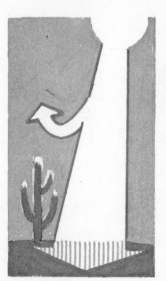

The sun's heat strikes the desert full-blast by day, but the heat escapes just as fast at night.

The cloud cover, water, and vegetation in temperate regions prevent extreme changes in temperatures.

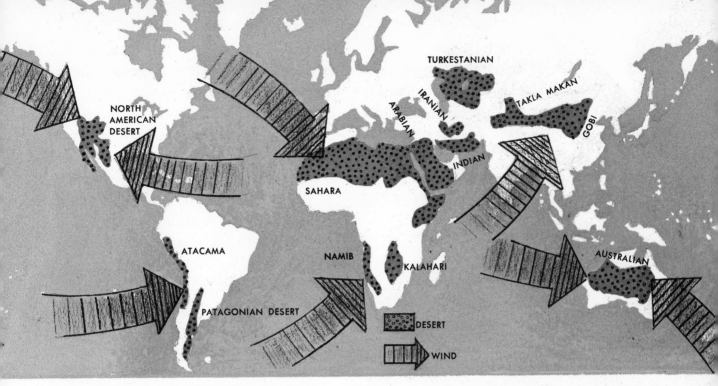

We show here the two desert belts within which the great deserts of the globe are located as well as the directions of the prevailing winds in these areas.

Since there are rarely any clouds in the desert sky, the surface of the ground and the lower strata of the atmosphere receive practically all of the direct radiation of the sun (about 90 per cent, while 10 per cent is deflected by dust particles). Consequently, air temperatures of 120°F. are not unusual; the surface of the ground often gets 30 to 50 degrees hotter.

When night falls, the situation reverses itself. The lack of insulating cloud cover (which lets all of the sun's radiation strike the desert full-blast during the day) allows 90 per cent of the accumulated heat to escape quickly into the upper air as soon as the sun sinks below the desert rim. Only 10 per cent is deflected down again by dust particles in the air. Temperatures may drop quickly 50 degrees and more between day and nightfall. The climate of the deserts is, naturally, influenced also by altitude and latitude. The higher above

sea level the desert is located and the farther away it is from the Equator, the colder the desert will be. The high Gobi Desert of Mongolia north of the Tropic of Cancer is the coldest desert, and the low-lying southern Sahara near the Equator, the hottest.

Generally speaking, there are 11 principal desert areas in the two arid belts that encircle our globe and comprise one-fifth of the earth's land surface.

Where are the world's great deserts?

Of these, the largest by far is the Sahara, which sprawls across the entire upper third of the vast continent of Africa — and then extends farther east to cover virtually all of the Arabian peninsula in Asia.

For the most part, the Sahara is a high, rocky tableland that is studded with gigantic boulders and cut up by gorges — called *wadies* — and low

7

rugged hills. In some places, it is covered by sparse grassy pastures on which the nomadic shepherds graze their flocks of sheep and goats.

Much of the Arabian desert, on the other hand, has the sort of landscape that we usually see depicted in the movies — mile after endless mile of shifting sand dunes that are sometimes hundreds of feet high.

South of the Equator in Africa lies the grim Kalahari Desert, almost as empty and desolate as the worst parts of the Sahara. The Kalahari, however, gets slightly more rainfall than most deserts, and contains some water holes that never completely dry up. Around these, the Bushmen, as the native pygmy tribes are called, build their flimsy villages of twigs and grass and live by killing the animals that come at night to drink. Their only sources of vegetable food are the roots of the desert shrubs that grow but sparsely in the hot and hostile climate.

Several hundred miles west of the Kalahari is the Namib Desert, which lies along the South African Coast and gets its moisture from the curious fogs that sometimes drift inland from the cold currents of the South Atlantic.

The Great Sandy Desert and the Great Victoria Desert in Australia make up the second largest desert area in the world. Occupying about half of that

The Great Wall of China runs along the southern edge of the Gobi Desert.

A camel caravan in the Sahara is on the way to a life-saving water hole.

great continent, the Australian desert stretches across large areas in Western Australia, South Australia, and the Northern Territory. Australians call it the "outback." Like the North American desert, and certain parts of the Sahara, the outback supports a sparse amount of grass, which allows the ranchers from "Down Under" to graze cattle and sheep upon it. But it takes many acres of such sparse desert land to sustain even one domestic animal.

In the southern part of the Soviet Union in Turkestan is a huge flat-floored basin sometimes called the Turanian Basin. Actually, it is the dried-up portion of the famous Russian *steppes*. Two deserts — the Kara Kum, or Black Sands, in the south and the Kyzl Kum, or Red Sands, in the north-east — form the heart of this basin. The *steppes* are something like our own Western prairies — level, treeless, but with a fairly rich soil that produces much of Russia's grain crops. Geologists believe that many thousands of years ago, these deserts, too, were productive agricultural land.

Oil pipelines now run through the Iranian desert, following the routes once used by trade caravans. The lives of the shepherds, however, have not changed much.

The great desert of northeastern Asia is the Gobi. The Gobi covers 500,000 square miles in Inner Mongolia, China, and Outer Mongolia. Whereas most deserts are boiling hot, the Gobi — situated as it is at a very high altitude — is freezing-cold, and is constantly swept by bitterly cold winds. These winds have blown away almost all traces of sand and soil, and left nothing behind but great rocks and boulders — as though a giant, in a playful mood, had scattered handfuls of giant pebbles over the desert floor. It was in the Gobi that the American explorer, Roy Chapman Andrews, found the first fossilized eggs of dinosaurs. As these prehistoric giant lizards could live only in a tropical climate, Andrews' discovery proved that at one time, many millions of years ago, the now-desolate Gobi was a steaming, humid jungle.

It was along the southern edge of the Gobi Desert that the Emperor Shih Huang Ti, about 200 B.C., ordered the Great Wall of China to be built as a protection from the Mongol armies that swooped down on China from the north. The Great Wall is one of the most fantastic structures ever created by man. It stretches for more than 1,500 miles, is some 25 feet high, about 25 feet thick at the base, and from 12 to 15 feet across at the top. Hundreds of thousands of laborers worked hundreds of years to build it. And it is said that the bodies of tens of thousands of workers who died on the job before it was completed were thrown into the wall and, like a sort of grisly cement, hold the stones together.

Before the Red Chinese isolated China from the rest of the free world, the Great Wall was one of that country's principal tourist attractions.

The Iranian desert and the Indian desert lie relatively close together. Like the desert of Arabia, the Iranian desert consists largely of shifting dunes of sand, many of which rise to 500 feet.

The Indian desert — sometimes referred to as the Thar — was once, thousands of years ago, an area of thriving towns and farmlands. But the patterns of the winds that blew over that part of Asia shifted. And over the centuries, the Thar valley dried up and became an arid wasteland of unproductive sand.

Among the major deserts of the world are the three long, narrow strips that run through South America: In Peru, the coastal area that extends from the Pacific Ocean to the Andes Mountains is largely desert; the 600-mile Atacama, in northern Chile, begins south of the border of Peru; and the Argentinian Patagonia is a barren tableland between the Andes and the Atlantic Ocean. Close to the sea, the few plants that these deserts sustain absorb most of their moisture from the sea air. Practically none of it is received in the form of rain. Indeed, statistics show that the Atacama has less rainfall than any other desert in the world. It is, however, rich in copper, gold, sulfur, borax, and sodium nitrate.

Water in the Desert

Two great rivers flow through the world's desert areas.

One is the storied Nile, which rises in the jungle-covered mountains around Lake Victoria in Africa and, the longest river in the world, flows 4,160 miles northward to empty into the Mediterranean Sea. Except for the narrow, fertile valley and the broad delta of the Nile, most of the rest of Egypt is a blazing, waterless desert.

The other is the mighty Colorado. Its source is a tiny stream high in the Rockies of Colorado, but it winds southward through North American desert land to the Gulf of California.

In all temperate lands, there is a vast reservoir of water that lies under the ground. This is known as the water table. Each time it rains, some of the water is held in suspension by the soil to feed the roots of growing plants, some is carried away by creeks and rivers, but most of it seeps down to a level where all the cracks and openings in the underlying rock are completely filled with water — which makes it practically always possible to reach water by digging a well.

What causes desert water holes and oases?

In the hottest deserts, however, such as the Arabian, for instance, the scant rainfall almost instantly evaporates in the heat of the sun, so no such water table exists. In some parts of the Saharan and Arabian deserts, it can happen that it rains not more than once in eight or ten years.

But even under these deserts flow a few underground rivers which may carry water from rainy areas hundreds, or even thousands, of miles away. Here and there, waters from these subterranean flows emerge to the surface of the desert in the form of a spring. In the Sahara, these springs are called "oases." In most other places, they are simply referred to as water holes.

It is around these oases that the Arabs build their desert towns — with clusters of fruit trees, flowers, grass, and palms gleaming like multi-colored jewels in the midst of the brown wasteland that surrounds them. And the few trails and roads that cross the desert go from one oasis to the next.

The same peculiar kind of flood that sometimes comes in the summer without warning occurs in the desert, especially in the American Southwest. They are called "flash" floods. For possibly 300 days out of the year, the sandy, rocky land is completely dry and arid. Then, by some freak movements of the winds high overhead, storm clouds suddenly gather and send down a deluge to drench the parched earth. The rain water which falls on the sun-baked earth in such great quantities and in such a short time rushes down the *arroyos* (as gullies are known in the American Southwest) in a vast wall of water that carries everything before it. Then, in a few hours, it is gone, having been greedily sucked up by the thirsty sand.

No experienced desert traveler will ever camp in what looks like a dry stream bed. For he knows that a "flash" flood may come roaring down the gully without warning and sweep away both him and his camp before he has even the slightest notion of what is about to happen.

Often, the desert plays weird tricks on the people who travel across it,

What is a mirage?

especially in the sandy reaches of the Sahara. A traveler, parched with thirst, may see a large lake of shimmering

11

Indescribable vistas (right) open up to the visitor from the Desert Watch Tower over the sweeping panorama of Grand Canyon.

Bryce Canyon in Utah (below right) once was a broad sandy plain before the many little rivers that flowed through it dissolved the limestone and left only the more durable rocks. Night view.

The Painted Desert (below) becomes alive with color at sunset.

DESERT HAWK IN FLIGHT

Sand-bearing winds carved the hole into the water-weakened sandstone which became the Natural Bridge in Navajo country, Monument Valley, Arizona.

The salt on the salt flats of Utah is packed down almost as hard as concrete.

This is the Petrified Forest in Arizona, where "... trees have been converted into jasper."

13

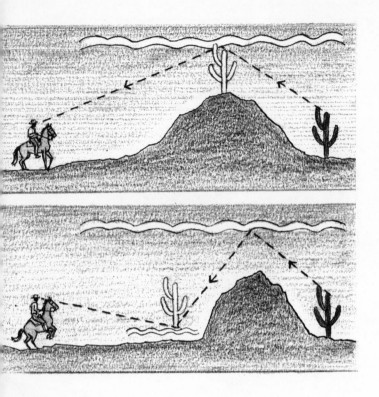

water about a mile away. As he struggles toward it, the lake retreats, changes its position, or disappears entirely. This, of course, was not a lake at all, but a mirage — an optical illusion. Frequently, houses and palm trees may appear on the shores of these "lakes." These are but the reflections of oases that may be many miles beyond the horizon.

A single mirage (above) and double mirage (below) occur when a layer of hot, moist air on an otherwise perfectly clear day acts like a mirror, just as calm water does in a pond. In the case of a double mirage, there is another layer of air which is cooler than the air higher up and acts like a second mirror.

The Face of the North American Desert

The desert with which most readers are familiar — if only from photos, movies, and TV shows — is the great American desert from west Texas through southern New Mexico, Arizona, and California, into southern Nevada and Utah. Its landscape, perhaps the most varied of any desert area in the world, matches the shifting sand dunes of Arabia, the rock-strewn wilderness of the Gobi, the semi-grasslands of the Australian outback, and offers the glorious beauty of the Grand Canyon, too. In respect to both plant and animal life, and because more of it has been reclaimed into productive land than in any other continent, it is the most interesting of all the world's desert regions.

At one time, hundreds of millions of years ago, what is today the American desert was a lush, dense jungle covered with prehistoric fern trees and early conifers. Dinosaurs and other long-extinct animals prowled through its rain-soaked trails. In the air above them flew the reptile-birds, the pterodactyls, vicious-looking close cousins to the monstrous dinosaurs, with wings of bare skin like bats.

The earth, which is always changing, was changing more rapidly and more drastically than it is today. New mountain ranges, the Rockies and the High Sierras, rose up, other areas became depressed, and what had once been a jungle became a great inland sea. When the waters flowed in over the forests, all plant and animal life ceased to exist. For millions of years, the sea covered what had been forest and jungle. Then, internal pressures pushed this part of the earth's surface upward again, the seas gradually disappeared and dried up, and the heat of the sun turned their bare and muddy bottoms into a desert.

Now the winds began to blow away the sand and dust, leaving only the hard rock that lay underneath. Little streams began to come down out of the newly formed mountains. This slow but irresistible action of wind and water has produced the most spectacular scenic effects.

Perhaps the most awe-inspiring example

How do wind and water sculpture the desert?

is Bryce Canyon in Utah. At one time, this was a broad and sandy plain. But as millions upon millions of years went slowly by, the little rivers that flowed through it dissolved the limestone and left only the more durable rocks behind. Then, the winds, which are the true sculptors of nature, took over the job of making Bryce Canyon the scenic fairyland it is today (see p. 12).

The winds sandblasted the rocks with much the same effect of sandpaper rubbed across a piece of wood. The softer parts of the rock formations eroded away, and the harder parts remained. Spires, walls, cathedral-type domes, fantastic rock-bridges, and other weird wind-sculptured structures were left behind.

Not too far from Bryce Canyon is the

How was the Petrified Forest formed?

Petrified Forest of Arizona in Navajo and Apache country. Here, the desert is strewn with the trunks of ancient conifer trees that have been turned into beautiful gem-like stones of agate, onyx, and carnelian — a place where, as Lt. Whipple, an Army officer who explored parts of northern Arizona in 1853, described it, ". . . trees have been converted into jasper." (See p. 13.)

The Indians have legends which tell how the Petrified Forest was created. One of the most fascinating of these tales tells of a god who went hunting in the forest which grew at the site of the Petrified Forest and who wanted to make a fire to cook the game he had killed. The firewood, however, was too wet to burn and the angry god cursed the forest and changed it into stone.

What really happened millions of years ago was that when the new mountain ranges were formed through pressures and eruptions within the earth, the sea submerged the dense jungle of fern trees and giant pines. When the mountains cooled and the swirling dust settled into the subsiding waters to form silt, the minerals dissolved into the water and soaked into the fibers of the wood. Gradually, over the eons, as the wood itself decayed and rotted away, the minerals hardened into the same pattern as the original wood of the tree. Then the seas drained away, and the mud and ooze that was left behind was turned by the sun into desert. The winds blew the soil away in centuries of erosion and the trees — now turned into lovely stone — began to emerge into the sunlight once more.

About 1,500 years ago, the Indians who inhabited that part of Arizona built houses and temples with the petrified logs — many of which still stand or have been restored; Agate House, once the home of probably a chief or a temple to a god, is one of the most impressive of these buildings. To preserve this "natural wonder," and save it from souvenir-hunters, the area, in 1906, was made the Petrified Forest National Monument.

Even more breath-taking than Agate House or the hundred or so other ruins of dwellings are the thousands of stone trees that lie at random on the floor of the Petrified Forest, gigantic and beautiful jewels that reflect in a thousand hues and colors the brilliance of the desert sun.

What is the Painted Desert? The Painted Desert, in which the Petrified Forest is located, is another of Nature's wonderlands that tourists drive thousands of miles to see. By day, the Painted Desert looks just about like any other desert. But when the sun begins to sink westward over the desert's edge, the whole great sandy plain assumes every color of a vast rainbow. It is as though Nature, with broad strokes of a giant paintbrush, was changing the brilliant colors every minute — or even every second.

The flaming spectacle is created by the fact that the mineral contents of the sand reflect and refract the sun's rays in a million different hues, all at the same time. The Painted Desert, at sunset, is certainly one of the most exciting sights of Nature (see p. 12).

What made the salt deserts? In parts of Utah, Nevada, and New Mexico, we find desert regions where the ground is composed predominantly of salt, borax, gypsum, and some other minerals (like that of the South American Atacama). These are the bottoms of lakes and inland seas which dried up millions of years ago. The Bonneville Salt Flats, in Utah, are probably the most typical example of such a salt desert. The salt, packed down almost as hard as concrete, stretches for miles from horizon to horizon without a single sign of plant or animal life. The Flats, also called the Bonneville Speedway, make an ideal testing-ground for high-speed racing cars because the surface is so stable.

The salt of these lifeless deserts provide an industry of major proportions. Some of it is purified into ordinary table salt; the rest, into chemical substances such as caustic soda, borax, and gypsum.

The Great Salt Lake in Utah is among the last of the ancient desert seas that have not yet completely dried up. Its water contains more than 20 per cent salt, and is so dense that a human body cannot sink in it. Bathers — even people who could not swim a stroke in fresh water or in the ocean — delight in floating on the surface like a piece of wood. But when they come out, their skins are literally incrusted with a thin layer of salt. If you were to take an ordinary glass of water from the lake and let it stand in the sun until it evaporated, you would find more than an inch of pure salt remaining at the bottom of the glass.

Nobody who has seen the Grand Canyon of the Colorado River in Arizona will ever forget it. It is Nature's architectural masterpiece, on the world's most magnificent scale (see p. 12).

How was the Grand Canyon created?

When the great inland sea of the Southwest drained away eons ago, the Colorado Plateau area rose up very slowly as a flat tableland. Unlike what happened to the Northeast when the range of the jagged Rocky Mountains formed, the earth's crust did not buckle and fold as it rose. Instead, its elevation was so gradual that the layers of rock were hardly bent. And they are still almost horizontal, even though the top of the Plateau is now nearly a mile and a half above sea level.

When the Plateau first began lifting upward, a system of rivers flowing down from the mountains ran across it. Chief among these was the ancestral Colorado. The river, which today flows at the bottom of a magnificent gorge a mile deep, 217 miles long, and as much as 18 miles wide in places, did not flow on the top and wear its way down, and geologists believe that it never was much higher than it is now. As the land rose upward, the river running through it maintained just about its original level.

To make the point clearer, geologists have likened the Colorado Plateau to a gigantic layer cake, and the river to a cutting-knife. But instead of the knife cutting downward through the cake, the cake has pushed itself upward against the cutting-edge of the knife, while the knife itself has remained almost stationary.

Today, guides take tourists on sure-footed mules down the narrow winding trails that lead from the rim to the can-

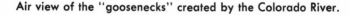

Air view of the "goosenecks" created by the Colorado River.

yon floor. If you ever take such a trip, you will see a living history book of the development of life on earth as you pass the fossil remains embedded in the various levels of the sedimentary rock.

At the bottom, you see the fossil remains of primitive algae, the first form of life which developed in the original sea. Then, higher up on the walls, you find the remains of primitive sea animals. After them come the amphibians, the first animals that left the sea and took up life on land. At last, higher up near the rim, are the traces of early ferns and primitive pine trees and the fossil tracks of the dinosaurs and other reptiles which roamed the Plateau when it was still jungle.

The Colorado River carries away thousands of tons of mud and sand every day. The Grand Canyon is still deepening, and most scientists have no doubt that the Colorado Plateau is still gently rising.

BEDOUIN WITH CHARACTERISTIC HEADGEAR

The People of the Desert

Man was never meant to live on the desert. But in all the wastelands of the world, he has learned to adapt himself to the harsh conditions that it imposes. However, unlike many desert animals, as we have seen, he cannot survive long without water. And so he has built an austere life around desert wells and water holes. Where water is plentiful, as it is in the valley of the Nile, the desert people have prospered. Where it is scarce, they have barely managed to survive.

The Negroid people of the Kalahari in Africa and the Australoid aborigines of the outback in Australia get along better with the desert than do people of Caucasian stock. This is because the heavy pigmentation of their skin offers them a certain amount of protection against the blazing sun. Thus, these darker-skinned inhabitants of the deserts of Southern Africa and Australia can go virtually naked in the sun, while

the people of the Saharan, the Arabian, and the Asian deserts have to bundle themselves up in heavy robes and garments of woolen or camel's hair cloth.

The Bedouins of the Sahara are nomad shepherds who live today much as they did a thousand years ago. They have no permanent homes. Their only possessions are their flocks of sheep and goats, their tents, their camels, and their horses. Because desert pasturage is sparse, and the pastures and wells are far apart, the Bedouin tribes keep constantly on the move. Unless they find a particularly good piece of grazing land, they rarely stay in one place more than a week, and usually change campsites every day or so.

How do the Bedouins live?

These wandering tribes may consist of as many as 50 or 100 people. The women and girls do the cooking and primitive housekeeping. They milk the sheep and goats, shear them, and weave cloth for tents and clothing from their wool. Camels are never shorn to provide material for the heavy camel's hair cloth that is the Bedouin's favorite. The camel keeps shedding hairs constantly, and women and children collect the hair the camel loses. Naturally, when a camel dies, the wool is shorn from its skin. The skin itself is used to make boots, saddles, and other leather goods.

The desert camel has a strange peculiarity. It can carry immense loads without showing any sign of exhaustion. When it finally comes to the end of its endurance, it simply topples over and dies. This fact is probably the origin of the saying, "the straw that broke the camel's back."

The men and boys of the Bedouin tribes tend the flocks, and the chieftains range far and wide on their swift horses in their endless search for new pastures.

The Bedouin's diet is a simple one. It

The Bedouin tent (above), made of material woven of goat hair, is always pitched with its entrance downwind for protection against treacherous sandstorms. It is stretched over light poles and often has rugs on the floor.

Bedouin herdsmen (picture at left) gather at a desert water hole. The camel is their treasured possession. It not only serves as a means of transportation, but is also a source of milk and meat. The hair, too, is used — for the weaving of materials.

During "cooler weather," the Tuaregs live in leather tents; during "heat waves," they build *zeribas*, makeshift huts of dried grass, for shelter. The men, not the women, wear veils over their faces.

consists mainly of a stew of camel's meat, or mutton, and small dumplings of cereal dough, which the tribes trade for in the desert towns. Sheep's eyeballs are considered a great delicacy. Eating utensils are unknown. The dish of stew is placed on the floor of the tent, and the family takes turn dipping into it with their fingers. As beverage, the Bedouin serves a small cup of coffee so strong that most Europeans find it extremely distasteful and difficult to drink.

Sometimes, when camped near a large oasis, the Bedouin is able to vary his diet with fresh fish. Strangely enough, these fish somehow manage to swim up the underground rivers that flow beneath the desert, and are caught in the wells and irrigation ditches surrounding the oasis.

The nomad's tent is a very simple structure, consisting of no more than a square of tightly woven wool or camel's hair, pegged down over poles and open at one end. The sandy floor is covered with woolen rugs on which the family sleeps. There is usually no other furniture.

The clothing of the Bedouin is as simple as his home, and is designed to protect him from the Sahara's extremes of intense heat and intense cold. Over a shirt and baggy pants, he wears a hooded cloak, or burnoose. It is wind-, water-, dust-, and sun-proof. He wears a turban-like hat that has a sort of heavy veil in the back. This either protects his neck from the sun, or can be used to cover up his face if the dust is heavy. On his feet, he wears slippers or light boots.

The Bedouin wraps his burnoose around him like a blanket at night. And if he is caught away from his tent by a sudden sandstorm, he sits on the ground and pulls his burnoose over his head to form a miniature tent while riding out the storm.

Aside from his flocks, which give him his livelihood, the nomad's two most important animals are camels and horses. The camels carry the tents and supplies from camp to camp, as well as the women and children. The men — especially the chieftains — ride swift Arabian horses.

The Bedouin is a hard worker, as he must be. He tends his flock and, like all nomads, is a good hunter. He likes to hunt the gazelles and game birds that run wild over the northern portions of the Sahara. He always hunts on horse-

TUAREG CHILD

TUAREG ZERIBA

back, shooting the gazelles with his rifle while the horse is on a dead run. He often hunts with falcons, as his ancestors have done for hundreds of years. When game is sighted, the falcon is released to flash into the air, swiftly catch up with the prey, and grab it in razor-sharp talons.

Such game birds and gazelle hunts provide a welcome change from the nomad's usual diet of goat meat or mutton.

Who are the blue-veiled Tuaregs?

Deep in the heart of the Sahara, in a region so dry that it often does not rain from one year's end to the next, live a strange group of Moslem tribesmen known as the Tuaregs. Of all Moslems, it is the Tuareg men, and not the women, who wear veils over their faces.

These veils — like their long, flowing robes and wrap-around turbans — are made of thin cotton dyed with the wild indigo that grows in desert oases. Being a primitive dye, it easily rubs off, so that the Tuareg's skin is a permanent purplish-blue color.

No Tuareg male ever displays any part of his face except his eyes. Even when he eats, he holds the veil out with his left hand and passes the food up underneath it.

Tuaregs graze their herds and cultivate small plots of land around the oases in their remote part of the desert. But they consider themselves to be above any kind of physical work. Instead, they keep Negro slaves who do all the manual labor, even saddling the Tuaregs' camels. The camels they ride are thin

21

and swift, not like the awkward beasts that carry the loads of caravans. These so-called racing-camels can cover incredibly large distances at relatively high speeds, and, unlike ordinary camels, move at a graceful, untiring gait.

Curiously enough, many of the Tuareg ornaments are in the form of a cross, and the men carry long, straight swords not unlike those of the ancient Christian Crusaders. Since the Tuaregs are lighter-skinned than most dwellers of the Sahara, these circumstances have led many people to speculate that they may indeed be the descendants of lost Crusaders who wandered deep into the desert and were unable to find their way back to the Christian armies.

Until the early 1900's, when they were more or less subdued by the French Legionnaires, the Tuaregs were known as the "desert pirates." They preyed on caravans, invaded the oases of other Arab tribes, stealing camels and anything else of value they came across. But today — although no less picturesque — they make their living by conducting caravans across the desert, and from the proceeds of their oases-farms. They are, however, still slave-owners, and few foreigners ever get far enough into the desert to change their curious way of life.

A strange people, the Mozabites, are the merchants of the **Who are the** desert. And they are **Mozabites?** the wealthiest of all the Saharan tribes.

Something like a thousand years ago, they were prosperous merchants in the cities along the Mediterranean coast.

Then they were persecuted by other Arab tribesmen for their heretical religious views and forced to flee into the vastness·of the desert. They did not go one at a time, but migrated as a group.

Deep in the desert, they finally found a refuge in one of the loneliest stretches of the Sahara. There were no wells, no surface water, and no oases. But they managed to dig deep down through the granite rock under the sand and to strike an underground river. They named their original town Ghardaïa, and it is still the center of the Mozabite culture.

The Mozabites owe their wealth and prosperity to the fact that their young men go out from Ghardaïa to all the cities of northern Africa, as well as those of southern Europe, and set·themselves up there as merchants and traders. A young Mozabite may be gone from his home for as long as 25 or 30 years while he makes his fortune. Then his son, or another young man from the village, goes away to take over the business he has established.

A young Mozabite wife often does not see her husband again after he leaves until they are both old people. The women are further enslaved by the fact that a woman seldom leaves the inside of her house, even to walk about Ghardaïa. But once the husband has returned from his business, rich and prosperous, the two settle down into a comfortable old age.

Most of the world's deserts have only one type of native living on them. But there are more assorted cultures in the Saharan-Arabian desert than there are varieties of landscapes.

Street scene in the "mud city" of Kano.

The Fulani and Hausa live in the northern part of Nigeria, which is the southern part of the Sahara. They are Moslems, too, and nomadic herdsmen who keep their flocks of sheep and goats constantly on the move from one sparse desert pasture to another. The men of both these tribes are spectacular horsemen, and pride themselves on the spirited Arab horses upon which they love to race like the wind over the desert and through their towns and villages.

The largest city in this part of the Sahara is Kano, which is literally a "city of mud." The older part of the city is surrounded by a massive mud wall, which is 30 to 40 feet thick. The low single-storey houses — some round and some square — are also made of mud. The mud is molded around roof beams and doorway supports made of palm tree trunks. On the occasion of a rare rain, the houses are repaired and renewed with fresh coats of mud plaster.

For centuries, Kano was an important crossroads for camel caravans which traveled between the northern desert and the jungle towns of Black Africa. The colorful camel trains still pass through, although much less frequently. The airplane has replaced the "ship of the desert," and Kano, having one of the largest airports in Africa, has become a vital center of airline travel.

Another Saharan tribe are the Teda. They live far down in the southeastern part of the Sahara. Because of their isolation, they have retained their ancient way of life to a greater extent than have most other dwellers in the Sahara. They seem to be more resistant to heat and lack of water than the other African nomads.

The Teda men, and women, are tough, fierce fighters. Before a young man can prove himself worthy of marriage, he must steal a camel from another tribe. Camel-stealing is a serious crime; he can be severely punished, if not put to death, in the event he is caught in the act.

The Chamba, unlike many other nomadic tribes, adapted quickly when the French took over the administration of

23

most of the Sahara. They became the principal members of the famous Camel Corps desert police force. They also took advantage of the French offer to educate their children. As a result, many Chamba today hold government administrative positions, while others became farmers around the oases towns.

Almost all of the Arabian peninsula is covered by one great desert of shifting sand dunes, few oases, and little or no vegetation. For almost all of history, most of the Arabs led backward, impoverished lives. Only their local sheiks who owned the larger oases lived in anything remotely resembling luxury. Then, European geologists found vast deposits of oil under the desert sands, and almost overnight, the way of life changed.

The sheiks still own all rights to the oil, and their personal fortunes have become incredible, with royalties often running to several millions of dollars a day. Only some of these local rulers have spent oil money for the benefit of the people by building roads, homes, schools, universities, and irrigation projects. But many Arabs have found well-paying jobs in the hundreds of oil fields that have sprung up all over the desert.

Far south of the Sahara, below the African jungle belt, lies the

Who are the Bushmen?

bleak Kalahari Desert. And here lives one of the most primitive of all people — the Bushmen — whose culture is little removed from that of the Stone Age. Although no count has ever been accurately made, it is estimated that they number only about 10,000.

Unlike the people of the Sahara, who bundle themselves up in heavy clothes as protection against both the heat and cold, the Bushmen go practically naked. The hot sun does not seem to have any effect upon them; and in the cold nights, they huddle together around small fires for warmth.

There is some scraggly plant life throughout most of the Kalahari, enough to attract small herds of game such as ostriches and antelopes. But even though the game is rare, the Bushmen hunt it relentlessly with crude spears and poison-tipped arrows. During especially dry seasons, when almost all of the game is gone, the Bushmen eke out a living by digging up roots of tuberous plants, and eating the insects they can catch.

There are always a few water holes in the Kalahari, and it is around these that the Bushmen make their temporary camps. A house is little more than a lean-to of sticks and grass.

Ostrich eggs are a great delicacy to the Bushmen. They punch a small hole in the eggs, suck out its raw contents, and carefully preserve the shells. When the water holes are full, they fill these shells with water and bury them deep in the sand, coming back to dig them up again in times of extreme dryness. When a Bushman, out on a hunting trip, comes to a dry water hole, he scoops out a depression with his hands. If water is close enough to the surface to make the sand damp, he patiently sucks up a little water through a hollow reed, a drop or two at a time.

The Bushmen are wards of the Government of the Union of South Africa, and in times of the most severe droughts,

The Bushmen's life is not very different today from the life of Stone Age people thousands of years ago. The huts are primitive shelters of twigs, and hunting is done with bows and arrows and spears. Ostrich eggs are still prize finds, as not only are they a delicacy, but the shells can be used for hoarding water.

The Bindibu lap up water like animals. They wouldn't know what a cup is.

caravans frequently make their way into the desert with enough supplies to prevent wholesale starvation. But for the most part, the Bushmen are content to live out their harsh and lonely lives without any contact with the rest of the world.

Where do the Bindibu live? Even more closely related to Stone Age man are the Bindibu people who are native to the great Australian desert. Literally, they possess nothing — they raise no crops, they wear no clothes, they build no homes, they have no herds, and they even have no utensils from which to eat or drink. Their only tools are crude spears and knives made from flint.

Like the Bushmen of the Kalahari, they are not affected by extremes of daytime heat and nighttime cold. They hunt together in small bands and keep always on the move, following the pattern of the scant desert rains because they know that beyond the rains will lie shallow pools of water. Although these pools dry up quickly, they provide drink for the Bindibu and tend to attract desert animals. Since they have no cups or other devices for drinking or storing water, the Bindibu crawl out into a shallow pool on all fours and drink like animals. And it is a rare treat for the tribe when the Bindibu hunters manage to kill a kangaroo or that odd ostrich-like bird, the emu, with their spears. When game is scarce, as it usually is, they subsist on roots, grubs, and worms.

The only concession the Bindibu make toward creating shelter for themselves is to use large clumps of dried grass as windbreaks while they sleep.

So apart from civilization do these primitive people live that it was only a relative few years ago that explorers discovered their existence.

Who inhabits the Asian deserts? Two thousand years ago, the Mongols were dread warriors who swept through Asia, and even into Europe, killing and plundering as they went. Today, they are dwell-

Mongols in the Gobi Desert have pitched their *yurt* after arriving at a new pasturage.

ers of the Gobi, one of the harshest desert areas in the world. It is certainly the coldest, located as it is on a flat and rocky plateau several thousand feet above sea level and far away from the Equator.

The Gobi is almost bare of vegetation, except for a scattering of wind-swept meadows on which a sparse grass grows. Here, the Mongols — riding stunted, furry horses — tend their herds of yaks, and manage to scrape a meager living from the barren land.

The Mongols live in portable tents called *yurts* that are constructed of felt, fur, and skins stretched over slender poles. The *yurts* are easily transported from pasturage to pasturage.

Few scientists have ventured into the Gobi, but we do know that it was once a rich and prosperous land, with cities and temples that now rest in desolate ruin. Geologists believe that there are vast oil deposits under the Gobi. And although the desert lies behind the "bamboo curtain" of Red China, it is likely that this untapped mineral wealth may one day bring back a measure of prosperity to the primitive Mongol people.

Who lives on the Atacama? Aside from the Arab people of the Sahara, perhaps the most civilized desert-dwellers are the Indians of South America who live in the lofty Atacama. The Atacama is often called the "desert above the clouds," because parts of its harsh, cold, rocky, treeless plains lie many thousands of feet above sea level.

The desert Indians of the Atacama live in rough stone huts, and the llama, the curious relative of the camel, is their chief economic resource. They use it as a beast of burden, weave heavy, warm clothing from its wool, and eat its flesh.

Today, however, there are few Indians left in the higher regions of the desert. Not only have valuable minerals been found on the lower regions of the

Atacama, but today, the world's largest copper mine is located in the Atacama desert. All this has changed the way of life of the desert Indians, who more and more are finding industrial employment.

The Desert Indians of the Atacama live in rough stone huts. The llama is their chief livestock.

Who lives in the American desert? The desert-dwelling Indians of the American Southwest were for the most part very primitive people. They inhabited the semi-desert areas that surrounded the dead wastelands of salt and sand — where there was just enough scanty rainfall to allow them to raise small crops of corn and beans, and enough small rivers and water holes to attract game for their meat pots. Their villages were clusters of mud huts, called "hogans."

But some of these ancient tribes achieved a high degree of civilization. Most prominent among them were the Cliff Dwellers of Colorado, Arizona, Utah, and New Mexico. Their story is a strange one.

They carved out villages of stone, perched like eagles' nests hundreds of feet high on the sheer canyon walls. These cliff-side caves, the largest of which is in Mesa Verde National Park in Colorado, offered protection from wild animals as well as hostile tribes.

Until about 700 years ago, the dry desert country of southwestern Colorado was a good deal greener than it is now, with sufficient rainfall for a thriving agricultural economy. So the Indians cultivated farms on the tops of the mesas above their cliff cities. Under the shelves of the cliffs, they constructed stone buildings that were two, three, or sometimes, four storeys high. Many of them were true "apartment houses" and some had as many as 200 rooms. The

various levels of the cliff city were connected by stairways which also led to the farms above, and were surrounded by walls to keep children from falling down into the canyon several hundreds of feet below.

Many of the houses had springs of fresh water that seeped down through the layers of rock.

The Cliff Dwellers developed a highly organized system of industry. Those who did not work on the farms became skilled potters or weavers, while others made knives, hatchets, and spears from flint and quartz. Those who were talented as artists decorated the walls with curious paintings, carvings, and religious symbols.

By studying the growth rings of trees that grew during that period, scientists can determine almost to the year the date when the civilization of the Cliff Dwellers came to an abrupt end.

About 1270, a great drought struck this part of the Southwest. No rain fell. The crops withered and died. The grass dried up, and the rivers ceased to flow. This period of famine lasted for 20 years, during which time the Cliff Dwellers left their cities and moved south toward the Rio Grande, where they built *pueblos* that are still inhabited by their descendants.

Today, some of the desert Indians still live in miserable poverty, eking out a bare living with their flocks of sheep and goats. Other tribes, like the Zuni and Hopi, deal in the thriving business of making souvenirs which they sell to tourists.

Much of the ranchland in this part of the Southwest lies in semi-desert country, providing just enough tough desert grass to sustain beef cattle if they have plenty of acreage to graze over. So, to this extent, many of the ranch-owners and cowhands can be called dwellers of the desert.

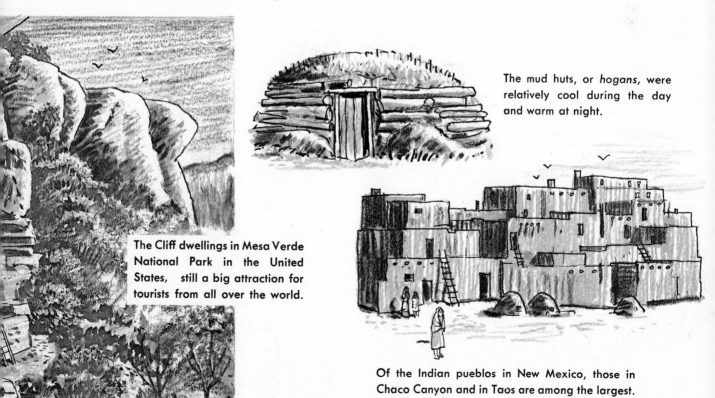

The mud huts, or *hogans*, were relatively cool during the day and warm at night.

The Cliff dwellings in Mesa Verde National Park in the United States, still a big attraction for tourists from all over the world.

Of the Indian pueblos in New Mexico, those in Chaco Canyon and in Taos are among the largest.

Plants of the Desert

PRICKLY PEAR CACTUS

Some of the oddest and most interesting plants in the world grow in the desert. Like all plants everywhere on earth, they rely on three sources of life: sun, water, and air. But as there is far too much sun and far too little water in the desert except for the oases, Nature has provided ingenious ways to compensate for this imbalance.

What are drought-evaders and drought-resisters?

A desert may lie brown and bare for a year, or two, or three. But scattered in the sand are the dormant seeds of the plants that flowered briefly during the last rainfall. Then, rain comes. And suddenly, almost overnight, the seeds come to life and the desert is covered with a brilliant carpet of flowers that often stretches as far as one can see — poppies, primroses, desert dandelions, verbenas, columbines, and phlox. Then, after a short while, at most a few weeks, the flowers shrivel and die after having dropped their own seeds, which in turn await the next life-giving miracle of rain. These kinds of plants can be called drought-evaders as they spring up only when it rains and evade the drought in the form of seeds.

Another mechanism of survival has developed in the drought-resisters, perennials which can store water. To this species belong the plants that we most frequently associate with the American desert, the cacti. They survive year in and year out and seem always a part of the desert landscape.

The cactus survives by storing water in its pulpy stem. Its root system is widespread and only inches below the surface so that the roots can instantly absorb the stingy rainfall before it is soaked up by the hot surface. The water is quickly drawn up from the roots into the plant, and after a rainfall, its pulpy stem can expand until 90 per cent of it may be water.

Then, after the rain has gone, the plant begins to live on the water that it has stored. As it uses up the water supply, its stems shrink in size and again appear shriveled and dead. But when the rains come again, the plant replenishes its "water-storage tanks," grows fat and plump once more, and puts out glorious clusters of blossoms that are the most exquisite in all the desert landscape.

Cacti come in a wide variety of shapes and sizes — from the giant saguaro, which can reach skyward for as high as 50 feet and live for 200 years, through the prickly pear, the hedgehog, the barrel, the pincushion, the beavertail cacti, down to tiny species that are no bigger in circumference than a penny. But they all store up water in much the same way. And many a thirsty traveler, caught in the desert without water, has saved his life by chopping off a cactus stem and squeezing out the liquid it contains.

To prevent evaporation of water, the leaves of most cacti plants have degenerated into thorny spikes, which at the same time protect the plant from browsing desert animals. But despite their formidable spikes, some cacti are the staple of diet for many of the smaller desert mammals.

The cholla cacti were given the name of the "jumping cholla" by some of the desert Indian tribes because they believed that its stems leaped out and grabbed anything that came near it. Obviously, the cholla can't do anything of the sort; its thorns simply stick tenaciously to anything, and its stems, which

JOSHUA TREE (THE LARGEST OF THE YUCCA FAMILY)

A "flash" flood in the desert may last only a few minutes, but at the same time, it may be a year's total rainfall.

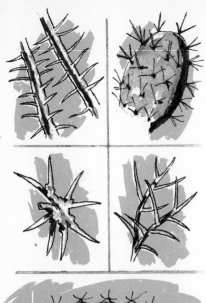

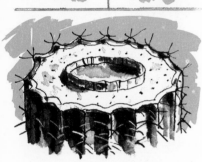

To prevent evaporation of water or to discourage animals from eating the plants, many desert plants have developed thorns. Top left, ocotillo barbs; right, prickly pear; below left, puncture vine; right, crucifix thorn.

Cross section through a saguaro showing the pulpy stem in which the plant stores water.

break off at the slightest touch, seem to leap from the plant to attach themselves onto whatever happens to brush against them.

Another curious desert plant is tumbleweed. It has very tiny roots, with branches which grow into a ball-like shape, often twice as large as an ordinary basketball. When it dies, the wind uproots it and sends it rolling and tumbling over the desert floor, enabling it to scatter its seeds for many miles around.

But not only cacti and tumbleweed grow in the desert. There are also trees. One of the most common desert trees is the mesquite, found in all but the driest areas. It grows in washes where the soil is deep and deposits of water can be found. The mesquite, too, is a drought-evader. It does not, however, store water but puts down an enormous system of taproots that search out the underground water and that have been reported to have penetrated to depths of 60 feet below the surface. A mesquite seedling is almost all root, and does little growing above ground until the roots have located a water supply.

Mesquite is very hard and dense and is much prized as firewood by cowboys and other people who spend much of their time on the semi-desert. On the other hand, it can become a great nuisance. In places where enough grass grows so that cattle can graze on the sparse clumps, mesquite becomes so thick that it crowds out the grass. Then it must be bulldozed away to allow the grass to come in again. But mesquite is one of the hardiest shrubs in the world, and the bulldozing process must be repeated every few years.

Many more species of plant life have adjusted to desert conditions. We have mentioned only a few, and have illustrated some others — just enough to show you that, however barren the desert may appear at first glance, somehow, somewhere, life hangs on.

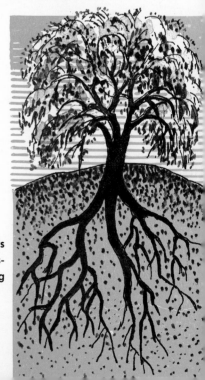

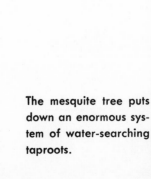

The mesquite tree puts down an enormous system of water-searching taproots.

SOUTH AFRICAN BLUE KLEINIA

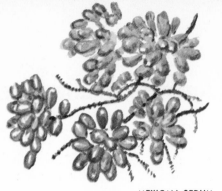

MEXICAN SEDUM

JUMPING CHOLLA

With the first rain, the plant seeds come alive and the desert is covered with a brilliant carpet of flowers. White daisies, purple *Nama*, yellow *Eriophyllum*, and many more start to bloom.

NIGHT-BLOOMING CEREUS

PRICKLY PEAR

MARIPOSA LILIES

BEAVERTAIL

HEDGEHOG CACTUS
IN BLOOM

BARREL CACTUS

Animals of the Desert

The one-humped Arabian camel lives in North Africa and Asia Minor.

The two-humped Bactrian camel is found in Central Asia from China to Turkestan.

Just as Nature in her wondrous way has adapted plant life to the rigors of the desert, so has she adapted animal life.

Does the camel store water in its hump?

Some of these animals — the desert tortoise, for instance — never really take a drink of water. They get the necessary moisture from the plants they feed on; others have been conditioned to go without water for long periods of time.

The animal that is most often associated with the arid areas is the camel, often called the "ship of the desert." It is the only domesticated desert animal, with the exception of the llama that lives in the high Andean part of the Atacama in Chile. The camel drinks about 25 or 30 gallons of water at a time, and then it can go without another drink for a week or two. When no water but green plant food is available, camels survive for months without drinking at all. They get, like many smaller desert creatures, all the moisture they need from their food. For centuries, even early scientists observing camels at a time when they were not yet domesticated believed that the camel had a hidden water-storage organ near the stomach, just as today many people still have the idea that the camel stores water in his hump. This, however, is a misconception. The hump is made up mostly of fat, collected when water and food are in abundance. From this reserve of fat in the hump, and the fat in other body tissue, the camel draws its energy during periods of little or no water and food. By breaking down this fat reserve within its body mechanism, the animal by a complicated chemical process produces the water the tissues need. By breaking down the fat, hydrogen is released within the body. The hydrogen combines with the oxygen the animal breathes to produce water within the body.

Shortly before the Civil War, the United States Army imported several hundred camels to serve as beasts of burden in the American desert. But the drivers, who were used to horses, mules, and oxen, did not know how to cope with the obstreperous camels, and the Camel Corps soon went out of existence. The camels were turned out to fend for themselves, and before long, all of them had disappeared.

Around the rim of the Australian desert live animals which **What are some typical outback animals?** cannot be found anywhere else in the world — the duck-billed platypus, a mammal that lays eggs; the koala, which looks like a child's teddy bear; the wombat; the flying possum. But only two species of animals live in the outback itself: the kangaroo (and his smaller cousin, the wallaby), and the common cottontail rabbit.

Oddly enough, the rabbits are not native to Australia, but were brought in by early settlers from England who missed seeing them around. But before too many years had gone by, the rabbit population had exploded, and the bunnies covered the desert in hordes of tens of millions. They ate up all the plant life, and nearly drank the water holes dry, leaving scant forage and water for the ranchers' sheep and cattle.

Mass rabbit hunts did little to reduce their number. Then, a few years ago, scientists introduced a disease called *myxomatosis,* which all but exterminated tnem. But some of them developed a resistance and an immunity to the disease, and now the cottontails are staging a slow but steady comeback.

Almost as much of a plague to the outback ranchers as the rabbits are the herds of kangaroos that roam over the desert. Like most of the animals native to Australia, the kangaroo is a marsupial, meaning that the mother carries her young in a pouch where it stays until it is weaned.

The Australian aborigines, natives of the outback, prize kangaroo meat as their favorite food. But as the kangaroos multiply faster than the natives can kill

PLATYPUS

FLYING POSSUM

KOALA

WOMBAT

KANGAROO

WALLABY

COTTONTAIL RABBIT

them, the ranchers wage constant war against these funny-looking "pests" to keep them from completely destroying their grazing lands.

The American desert sustains the greatest variety of wildlife of any of the world's desert areas, and the most interesting, as well. But life is a grim and never-ending struggle to stay alive. Some desert animals — small rodents, small birds, and insects — live on plants and seeds that give them water as well as food. The middle-sized animals — snakes, lizards, foxes, and, of course, the babies of every species — eat the smaller ones. And the big animals — the bobcats, coyotes, wild pigs, and badgers — feast on them

What are the typical animals of the American desert?

all, in turn, but need some water to supplement the liquids they get from their prey. So Nature has established an endless chain of life and death to provide for all its desert creatures.

We can describe, or illustrate, only a small selection from among those American desert creatures that are especially interesting. A list of just the names of the more than 5,000 species of insects, reptiles, birds, and mammals — and this would not include the many microscopic life forms which have adapted to desert conditions — would more than fill the pages of this book.

INSECTS

The desert teems with insects — crickets, locusts, beetles, and ants of a hundred varieties. These smallest of desert creatures need vegetation of some kind. They eat seeds, bits of leaves, and suck plant juice.

Of all the desert insects, the strangest is the pepsis wasp. She carries a poisonous stinger in her tail to fight off enemies. But she makes fantastic use of it — it provides her with a place to lay her eggs! The way she manages this creates more than a fifty-fifty chance of being

The pepsis wasp, also called "tarantula hawk," has subdued the large spider with a paralyzing sting.

The harvester ants store seeds; the honeypot ants have "living stores" of plant juice on which they feed during the drought periods.

killed by the tarantula. The pepsis wasp lays her eggs in the body of the largest spider of the desert, the fierce-looking, hairy tarantula.

When the pepsis is ready to lay an egg (she lays only one at a time), she has to find a tarantula. This is not too hard as all insects are the tarantula's natural food. The instincts of the two, wasp and spider, let them meet halfway, so to speak. The tarantula comes at the pepsis, eager to catch a snack. But now the pepsis puts up a fierce fight. If the spider bites her, she is finished. So, she fights cautiously. Her objective is to work her way under the tarantula and sting it in its soft underbelly, the only place her stinger can penetrate. If she succeeds, she stabs the tarantula. The poison does not kill the spider immediately, but paralyzes it completely. Now pepsis begins to dig a hole in the sand in which to bury her victim. This is difficult work, for the tarantula is several times her size. But when the chore is finally done, and the spider is buried, the wasp lays her single egg in its body, which provides the food for the young wasp larva which develops from the egg.

TOADS AND LIZARDS

There are several species of toads which live in the desert, feeding on insects and worms. One of the most interesting is the spadefoot toad. On each hind foot, it has appendages that it uses as digging tools. After the rains

The horned "toad" is actually a spiny lizard.

The spadefoot toad hibernates during the dry season.

FOOT

The gila monster is the only poisonous lizard in the American desert.

37

have gone and the desert begins to dry up again, it uses the spadefeet to dig backward into the ground and cover itself up.

There the spadefoot toad hibernates until it rains again, perhaps in ten or more months. At that time, the toad wakes up and goes to the nearest pool or puddle of water where it finds a female whose eggs it fertilizes. Soon, the tadpoles hatch out. Within three or four weeks, by the time the pools and puddles are dried up again, the young toads, now grown to maturity, dig themselves into burrows of their own. And so one of the desert's oddest life cycles goes on.

Other types of toads and frogs live around the edges of permanent water holes all the year round, resting in the shade of rocks by day, and coming out in the cool of the evening to catch with their long, sticky tongues any hapless beetle or centipede that may come wandering by. But the toad must be on the alert, too, lest it becomes the dinner of a hungry desert snake.

The "toad" that most people associate with the American desert, the horned "toad," is not really a toad but a spiny lizard. Its horns and spines give the lizard a dangerous and ferocious look to its enemies, but in reality, it is quick, gentle, and harmless. Visitors to the desert often catch horned "toads" and take them home as interesting pets.

Stories have been told about horned "toads" being found in hard deposits of dried-up mud where they have lain dormant for many years, to come alive again after being exposed to the air. But the chances are that the tellers of these tales have excavated a spadefoot toad and not a horned "toad."

Many kinds of lizards scuttle back and forth across the desert floor. For the most part, they live on insects, bugs, and the leaves of desert plants. But many bigger species of lizards eat the members of smaller species, thus keeping the "balance of desert life" while satisfying their appetites.

The largest of the lizards, the Gila monster, is also the only poisonous lizard in the United States. Its diet consists of rats, ground squirrels, and, of course, other lizards.

When the Gila monster nabs a victim, it hangs on and chews while the poison flows from its teeth. The monster is not aggressive if not hungry and will never attack a man. But on occasion, a careless person, groping with his hands under a rock, has had it seized in the Gila monster's bulldog grip. The poison is not venomous enough to kill a human, but it will make him miserably sick for a few days.

The chuckwalla is a desert lizard that protects itself by gulping in air, puffing up, and wedging so tightly between crevice walls that an enemy cannot pull it out.

Another big and fierce-looking lizard is the chuckwalla. But for all its ferocious appearance, it is extremely timid. When danger threatens, it scampers for the nearest rock crevice. There, it puffs itself up by gulping in air until it is wedged so tightly between the crevice walls that an enemy cannot possibly pull it out. The desert Indians, who value its meat, pierce its stomach with a sharp stick to deflate and get it out of its hiding place.

TORTOISES AND ARMADILLOS

The desert tortoise never drinks water. Instead, it stores up excess moisture from cactus leaves and other succulent plants in two sacs under its shell. Unlike most other desert creatures, it does not seem to mind being out in the burning noonday sun. Protected by a thick shell of armor, it has few enemies. The only way to get at it is to roll it over on its back; but then it has an undershell, too, into which it can pull its feet and head. So to most predators, the tortoise is not worth the bother.

The other armored creature of the desert is the fantastic-looking armadillo.

Actually, it is a throwback to prehistoric times. When danger approaches, it scurries for its burrow or, if that is too far away, it buries itself in the sand. If there is time for neither of these protective maneuvers — for the armadillo is a dull fellow with weak eyes and poor hearing — it curls up into an armored ball and hopes for the best.

Unfortunately, the armadillo has big wide ears that stick out from the shell. Thus, it is not difficult for a fox or a coyote to grab it by the ears, unwind it out of the armored-ball position, and use it as the main course of the evening meal.

THE DESERT RODENTS

Rats, mice, and ground squirrels are found all over the desert. By day, they lie in their burrows beneath the sand,

A tortoise nibbling at cactus leaves for food and water supply.

The armadillo can roll itself up when attacked.

39

GROUND SQUIRREL

WHITE-FOOTED MOUSE

PACK-RAT

KANGAROO RAT AND SIDEWINDER

KANGAROO RAT IN BURROW

The unusual movement of the sidewinder leaves ladder-like furrows in the loose sand.

but at night, they come out to do their harvesting of seeds and delicious bits of cactus stems. But they must be very cautious, for every meat-eating animal in the desert is their enemy. Of them all, the most amazing — in more ways than one — is the odd little kangaroo rat.

Although obviously no relation to the kangaroo of Australia, the kangaroo rat bears it a remarkable resemblance. Only about two inches long by two inches high, it has enormous hind legs with huge hind feet, tiny forepaws, and a tail three times as long as its body.

It moves by hopping, just as the Australian kangaroo does. And while a full-grown kangaroo may be six feet tall, weigh up to 200 pounds, and cover 20 feet in one bound, the tiny kangaroo rat can jump five feet in the same manner. Not only that, it can use its tail as a rudder and change course in mid-air.

This unusual little fellow, like almost all the desert rodents, drinks no water. Instead, it gets all the moisture its body needs from the seeds and bits of succulent plants that make up its diet. Foxes, snakes, hawks, bobcats, and owls, in turn, get much of their own water from the kangaroo rat's flesh.

Caught out in the open too far from its burrow, the little kangaroo rat is

POCKET MOUSE

JACK RABBIT

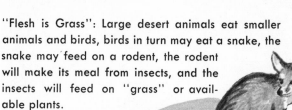

KING SNAKE

"Flesh is Grass": Large desert animals eat smaller animals and birds, birds in turn may eat a snake, the snake may feed on a rodent, the rodent will make its meal from insects, and the insects will feed on "grass" or available plants.

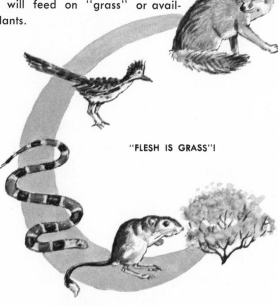

"FLESH IS GRASS"!

lucky to escape from these big predators alive. Against the desert rattlesnake, however, it has a most curious defense. Instead of retreating, as most animals do at a snake's approach, the rat turns and kicks up a shower of sand into the snake's face. Since snakes have no eyelids, this kind of assault is more than the rattler can take. So it slithers off in search of a meal that is a little less aggressive.

One of the few desert rodents that is a nuisance to man is the pack-rat. When it goes out at night to gather food, it carries the harvest home in pouches in its cheeks. And it is extremely attracted by any bright object it may come across. When it invades, as it often does, the cabin of a desert miner, or a lonely ranch-house, it will take along anything that happens to shine — including coins, spoons, and even watches.

To protect its nest from marauding meat-eaters, the pack-rat covers the entrance to its hole with prickly cactus spines. But the predators sleep by day and prowl by night, just like the pack-rat, so it is in the desert night that it's usually nabbed.

The other desert rodents — ground squirrels, pocket mice, white mice, deer mice, and their many cousins — all live on seeds and bits of cactus. But none have quite the odd peculiarities of the pack- or kangaroo rat.

DESERT SNAKES

The three most common snakes of the American desert are the king snake, the diamondback rattler, and the sidewinder. All prey upon rodents, birds,

birds' eggs, and lizards. The king snake also kills and eats rattlers.

Although not poisonous, the king is immune to rattlesnake poison. So when the two meet, the rattler usually beats a hasty retreat and escapes (if the king snake is not too hungry).

Both the king snake and the diamondback look very much like their close relatives in other parts of the South and West. But the sidewinder is unique to the American desert. It moves by swinging its body along sideways, one loop after another, which permits it to travel through soft, deep sand where other snakes are unable to go. The trail of a sidewinder looks something like the track of a huge tractor tire.

Only a few snakes move in this manner. The small sand viper of the Sahara is another.

The desert cobra, a beautiful but deadly snake, is found all around the edges of the Sahara, but never in the interior. While it likes the dry, barren sand of the desert, it never wanders very far from water. This is the cobra that was made the symbol of royalty of the ancient Egyptian kings.

One of the most poisonous snakes in the world is the tiger snake, which is found in the Australian outback.

The whippoorwill is a nocturnal desert bird that feeds on insects.

The road runner is one of the few desert animals that dares to fight with the dreaded rattler.

HEAD OF DESERT RATTLESNAKE

Very few humans have survived the bite of this snake for more than a few minutes without immediate medical attention — and even if anti-snakebite serum is injected at once, the poison very often proves fatal after a few hours.

DESERT BIRDS

The American desert abounds with birds. Most of them belong to the same species as the larks, woodpeckers, swallows, swifts, doves, quails, thrushes, wrens, orioles, and warblers of the woods and the fields. Somehow, they have managed to come to terms with desert life. As a rule, they build their nests in cactus stems and desert trees not far from water holes; the birds, while feeding on seeds and insects, still must drink water every day.

Birds cannot tolerate great degrees of heat. That's why they seek the cacti. The thorns provide shade as well as protection from roving predators.

Meat-eating birds like the owl and the red-tailed hawk, for instance, get

by wing feathers, the hawk often grabs the reptile's head with its powerful beak and kills it by breaking its neck.

The most curious bird of all in the American desert is the comical-looking road runner. Although its wings are weak, it can fly a little, but it rarely does except when in danger of being caught by a coyote or a bobcat. Full-grown, the road runner is about two feet long, with a topknot on his head and a long, white-streaked tail that juts up when the bird is alarmed.

The choicest item on the road runner's bill of fare is a nice juicy snake or lizard. Of the two, however, it prefers a snake, and a rattler, if possible. It kills the rattlesnake by pecking it to death with a long, sharp bill, all the time avoiding the snake's frantic strikes with deft and quick movements of the head.

Desert travelers tell stories of seeing a road runner ambling along at its clownish gait with a foot or more of snake hanging out of its mouth. If the snake is too long to be swallowed altogether, the bird digests it a little bit at a time, swallowing down more and more as the portions are consumed by its strong digestive juices.

Because of this odd dietary preference, the little road runner is perhaps the most effective snake-killer in the desert.

THE BIG ANIMALS

Most of the big carnivorous animals of the desert find their best hunting around the permanent water holes. Here, the timid little pygmy deer — that generations ago somehow wandered

most of their water supply from the flesh of the animals they prey upon.

Many owls build nests inside the stem of a cactus. But one species, the burrowing owl, usurps the underground hole of a ground squirrel for its daytime nest. At the approach of the owl, the squirrels scamper for safety; in the event of just such an emergency, the burrows usually have more than one entrance. But now the owl has a nice, cool home where it is protected during the long, hot days until it is time to go hunting in the cool of the night.

The desert hawk is a big, fearless bird that thrives on all sorts of rodents. It glides through the air in silent circles, rarely needing to move its wings until it spies a ground squirrel, a rat, or a mouse. Then it dives down, with great claws outstretched, and swoops up its prey before the victim knows what has hit it.

A hawk is not even afraid to attack a rattlesnake. The rattler, unlike a rat, however, can put up a fight. Protected to a certain extent from the snake's bite

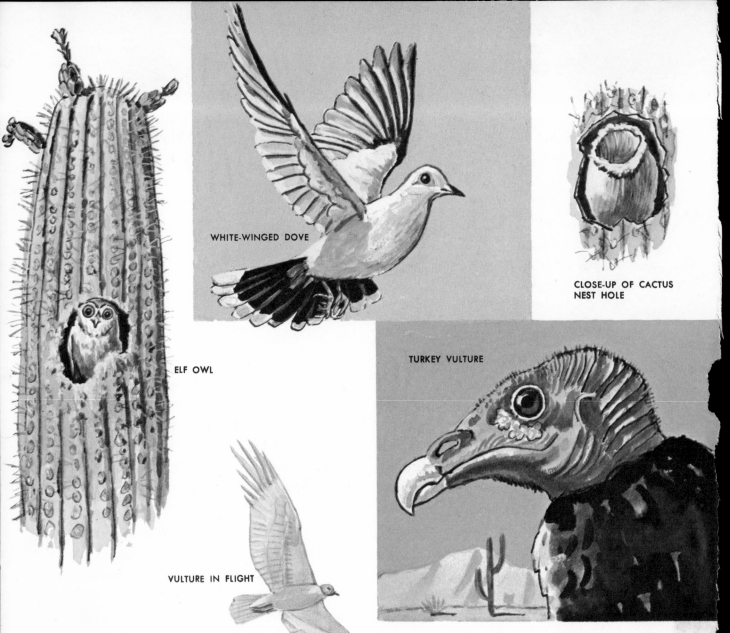

WHITE-WINGED DOVE

CLOSE-UP OF CACTUS NEST HOLE

ELF OWL

TURKEY VULTURE

VULTURE IN FLIGHT

The elf owl is the smallest of the desert owls. It hides during the day, often in the cactus nest holes of other birds, and hunts during the night. The white-winged dove migrates during the winter to Mexico where it feeds on the flowers and fruit in the saguaro cactus forests.

down out of the plains and mountains — come for their evening drink, and to feed on the plants which grow by the water. Their ancestors were full-sized deer, but in adapting themselves to the rigors of desert life, they have become dwarfed in size.

During the day, they stay in the shade of rocks to keep cool. When they begin to stir in the evening, they are the natural prey of such powerful meat-eaters as, for instance, the desert bobcat.

The bobcat will eat almost anything, from rats to ground squirrels. But if it has a choice, it prefers the sweet flesh of a young deer or a baby peccary. One such kill will provide several meals, making further hunting unnecessary this particular night.

The peccary is another denizen of the water hole. Long-snouted and pig-like, it is often referred to as a "wild pig," but it is not a pig at all, despite its outward appearance. Like a pig, it likes to wallow in the mud around the edge of the water hole. Peccaries, too, have wide-ranging appetites. They greedily eat cactus fruits, toads, the eggs of any birds that have imprudently built their nests too close to the ground, snakes, lizards, rats, squirrels, and even the roots of desert plants. They have long, sharp tusks, short tempers, and are afraid of nothing.

Almost all desert animals give the peccaries a wide berth, for they usually travel in small herds and are more than a match for anything that might get a notion to attack them. It is only when a youngster wanders away from the herd that a bobcat or a coyote will attempt to kill a peccary for dinner.

The ring-tailed cat is really a first cousin of the common raccoon. But like

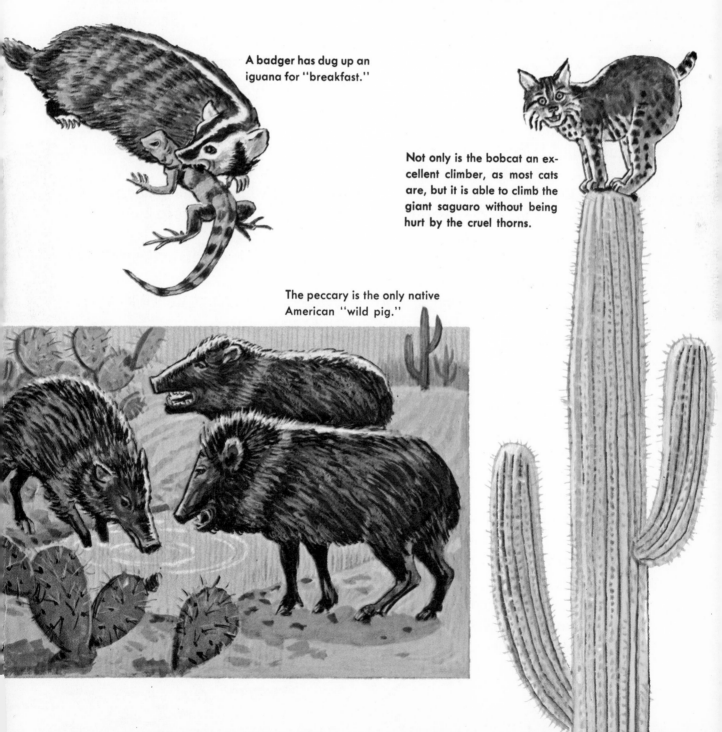

A badger has dug up an iguana for "breakfast."

Not only is the bobcat an excellent climber, as most cats are, but it is able to climb the giant saguaro without being hurt by the cruel thorns.

The peccary is the only native American "wild pig."

The kit fox is a swift night-hunter of rodents. Its huge ears help to detect the slightest scampering of its prey.

a cat, its favorite food is the rodent, especially the kangaroo rat. (Actually, the funny little kangaroo rat is almost the staple food for all the meat-eaters of the desert.)

The spotted skunk of the desert is one fellow that no other animal wants to fool with. When the skunk comes to the water hole for its nightly drink, all the others retreat to a safe distance. For, like its relatives in almost all other parts of the United States, it can squirt out a spray of pungent, oily, evil-smelling liquid from glands beneath the tail. Because of this unique defense, the skunk has few enemies in the desert, except perhaps a rattlesnake which might surprise it with its "tail down." So the skunk contents itself with living a peaceful life, living off an endless supply of rats, mice, and baby squirrels, with an occasional tidbit of cactus fruit or berries for "dessert."

The kit fox looks almost exactly like his cousin from far across the sea, the desert fox of the Sahara. It has often been called the cutest and most appeal-

ing member of the entire canine family because of its soft, furry body and enormous ears. Like most of the other desert animals, it depends largely on the rodents for its "daily bread," although now and then it enjoys the flavor of a desert song bird or a road runner.

"Singing" the evening song of the American desert is the coyote, also called the prairie wolf, brush wolf, or desert wolf or, by its Latin name of *Canis latrans,* meaning "barking dog." Leaving its lair after sundown and sitting down on a nearby knoll, alone or in the company of other coyotes (it likes to hunt in pairs), it will fill the air with its mournful howl. The cries of one single animal will sound like those of a whole pack, ranging from short yaps, barks, and whines to the finale, a howl that fills the quiet air for an enormous distance.

The coyote is cousin to the wolf and to the dog. As a rule, it is a scrawny, mangy-looking animal even if kept well-fed in zoos.

Jack rabbits and road runners are the coyote's special favorites. But both are troublesome to catch. The road runner, because of its speed and evasive tactics, can usually leave the coyote exhausted and howling with disappointment. The desert jack rabbit, running in tremendous leaps, can outdistance the coyote. But the rangy jack, like the cottontail bunnies that we see all over the United States, hates to wander too far from its home, and so it runs in circles. Often the coyote lies in wait and grabs the rabbit the second time around.

If it fails to catch a jack rabbit or a road runner when it is hungry, a few juicy ground squirrels or kangaroo rats will fill the "bill of fare" nicely. And when it can bring down a delicious mule deer fawn, that is a special occasion.

Coyotes never harm people. They are widely hunted because they are considered wholesale destroyers of sheep and other small livestock. This, however, is very much an exaggeration, and actually, the coyote does more good as a destroyer of rodents than it does harm as a destroyer of livestock.

Man and the Desert

The best example of a man-made desert was the famous Dust Bowl of the 1930's in Oklahoma. For years, this had been fertile grass country providing plentiful graze for thousands

How can man create a desert?

of head of cattle. Then farmers plowed up the grass to plant crops, and thus destroyed the thick carpet of grass roots that held the soil in place and retained water in the earth.

Then came a long period of drought and high winds that blew the soil away in great sandstorms. The dust and lack of water soon destroyed what was left of the crops, and covered the land with a blanket of dust that was in places several feet thick, thus turning it into a true desert waste.

Most of the farmers left their land which could not support them any more; only a few of the hardier, and wealthier, ones stuck it out. Today, with the help of the United States Department of

The Oklahoma Dust Bowl of the 1930's, a picture of despair and hopelessness.

Millions of acres of land have been reclaimed with irrigation, which transformed desert regions into bumper-crop producing farmland.

Agriculture, the dismal Dust Bowl is slowly being turned once again into productive farming and grazing land.

Some of the richest farmland in the world is in the Imperial Valley in southern California and produces bumper crops of fruits and vegetables the year around. Yet, only a few decades ago, it was as dry and desolate as the worst parts of the Sahara.

How can man reclaim the desert?

This magical transformation came about when water from the lower Colorado River was diverted across the grim Sonoran desert into the valley by means of a concrete-lined canal that carried millions of gallons each day. Spread throughout the valley by means of irrigation ditches, the water soon turned the arid sand into fertile soil, making it a man-made oasis in the midst of the unproductive desert that still surrounds it. Each year, more and more of the American desert is being reclaimed by such irrigation. Scientists are also perfecting atomic-powered plants to refine sea water, and thus provide an endless source of fresh water for future irrigation projects.

Actually, the principle of irrigation is not new. It was first used successfully 2,000 years ago by the Phoenicians in the Negev desert of the Holy Land for the cultivation of grain and fruit. But after the Moslem armies conquered the country, the irrigation projects were neglected and the Negev quickly reverted to worthless desert again.

In 1948, this wasteland became a part of the new nation of Israel. And Israeli engineers began at once to reclaim the Negev. As of today, they have reclaimed nearly 1,000,000 acres of the useless Negev into prosperous grazing and farming land.

Looking ahead into the future, and considering the giant steps that modern science is taking — for example, the de-salting of sea water, and projected methods of controlling rainfall — it is possible to foresee that, one day, all of the desert wastes of the world will be transformed into blooming gardens to feed the world's exploding population.